MW01078461

To

_____

From

_____

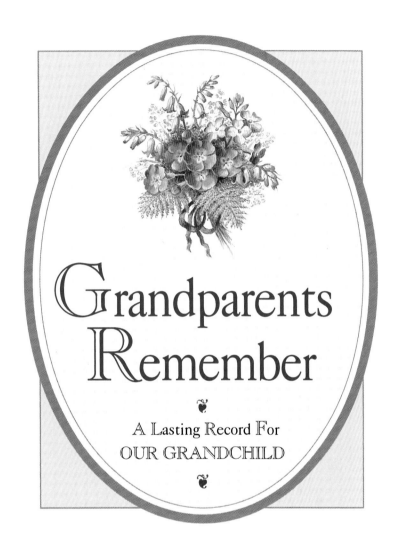

Grandparents Remember

A Lasting Record For
OUR GRANDCHILD

Victoria Avenue
PAPER COMPANY

Victoria Avenue Paper Company
A division of The Five Mile Press Pty. Ltd.
22 Summit Road
Noble Park Victoria 3174 Australia

First published 1991
This edition first published 1995
Reprinted 1996
Illustrations and design © The Five Mile Press Pty. Ltd.
Test Illustrations by Margie Chellew
Front cover floral bouquet by Shirley Barber
Cover floral pattern by Wendy Straw

Made in China

Introduction

Important details of your family history can easily be lost and forgotten unless you make a conscious effort to write them down. This book will help you set out your wealth of recollections in a logical and readable format.

When you have filled it in, it will become much more than a decorative and entertaining gift — it will be a unique collection of personal memories, and an invaluable record about your family. In time, it may even become a treasured heirloom to be passed down from generation to generation.

So fill it in with love and care, and add as many favourite photographs, family mementoes and interesting documents as you can. This is a very special gift — not just for your grandchild, but for future generations of your family.

Contents

Contents

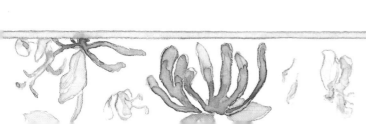

Your Mother's Family Tree

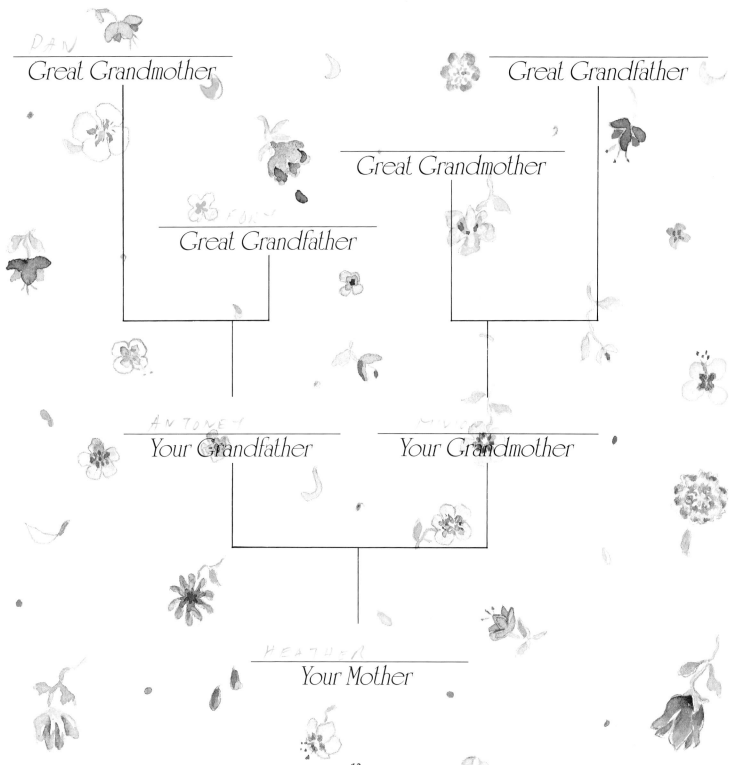

DAN
Great Grandmother

Great Grandfather

TONY
Great Grandfather

Great Grandmother

ANTONEY
Your Grandfather

Your Grandmother

HEATHER
Your Mother

Your Father's Family Tree

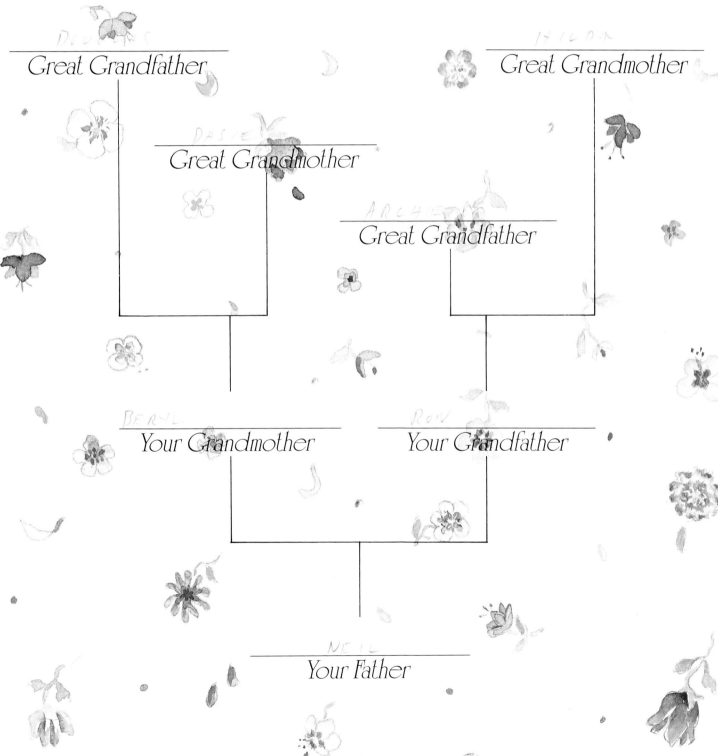

DOUGLAS

Great Grandfather

HILDA

Great Grandmother

DAISY

Great Grandmother

ARCHIE

Great Grandfather

BERYL

Your Grandmother

RON

Your Grandfather

NEIL

Your Father

"Grandmother"

Arabic: *Sitt*
Bulgarian: *Baba*
Chinese: *Zu-mu*
Danish: *Farmor, Mormor*
Dutch: *Oma*
English: *Grandmother, Grandma*
Grandmama, Granny
Nana, Nanny
Fiji: *Bu*
Finnish: *Isoäiti, Mummi*
French: *Grand-mère*
German: *Grossmutter*
Greek: *Yiayia*
Hawaiian: *Kupuna wahine, Tutu*
Hebrew: *Savta*
Hungarian: *Nagyanana*
Irish: *Mama, Seanmháthair*
Italian: *Nonna*
Japanese: *Oba-San*
Koori: *Bargi, Bakkano, Maiyanowe*
Korean: *Hal Mo-ni*
Maori: *Kuia*
Norwegian: *Farmor, Mormor*
Papua New Guinean: *Lapun Mama, Tumbuna*
Polish: *Babcia*
Portuguese: *Avó*
Romanian: *Bunica*
Russian: *Babushka*
Spanish: *Abuela, Abuelita*
Swedish: *Farmor, Mormor*
Thai: *Yai, Taa*
Turkish: *Büyük anne*
Vietnamese: *Bà*
Welsh: *Mam-gu, Nain*
Yiddish: *Bobe*

"Grandfather"

Arabic: Jad
Bulgarian: Dyado
Chinese: Yeye, Zufu
Danish: Morfar, Farfar
Dutch: Grootvader, Opa
English: Grandfather, Grandpa
Grandad, Gramps
Fiji: Tai
Finnish: Isoisä
French: Grand-père
German: Grossvater
Greek: Papous
Hawaiian: Kupuna kane
Hebrew: Saba
Hungarian: Nagyapa
Irish: Seanathair
Italian: Nonno
Japanese: Ojíi-san
Koori: Nerbungeron, Ngaityapalle,
Pola, Tipi, Ulwai
Korean: Harabugi
Maori: Koroua
Norwegian: Bestefar
Papua New Guinean: Lapun Papa, Tumbuna
Polish: Dziadek
Portuguese: Avô
Romanian: Bunic
Russian: Dyedushka
Spanish: Abuelo
Swedish: Morfar, Farfar
Thai: Yaa, Poo
Turkish: Dede
Vietnamese: Ông
Welsh: Tad-cu
Yiddish: Zayde

Grandmother's Grandparents
MATERNAL

My Grandfather's Name

DAVID CAMBRELL

My Grandmother's Name

SARA JONES

My Grandparents Met

They Were Married

When   Where

They Lived At

My Grandfather Earned His Living

ELECTRICIAN

Grandmother's Grandparents
PATERNAL

My Grandfather's Name

JOHN BLACKSTOCK

My Grandmother's Name

My Grandparents Met

They Were Married

When   Where

They Lived At

My Grandfather Earned His Living

FARMER & CITY WORKS CREW

Grandfather's Grandparents
MATERNAL

My Grandfather's Name

GEORGE   BARBER

My Grandmother's Name

MARY

My Grandparents Met

They Were Married

When   Where

They Lived At

My Grandfather Earned His Living

MINE ENGINEER

Grandfather's Grandparents
PATERNAL

My Grandfather's Name

GEORGE MCKEEVER

My Grandmother's Name

MARY

My Grandparents Met

They Were Married

When   Where

They Lived At

My Grandfather Earned His Living

BAKER

19

Grandmother's Parents

My Father's Name

DOUGLAS FRANCES

My Mother's Name

(DASIE) MARGARET CAMPBELL CAMPBELL

My Parents Met

My Father's Work

ELECTRICIAN

My Mother's Work

HOME MAKER

Grandfather's Parents

My Father's Name

ARCHIE

My Mother's Name

HILDA

My Parents Met

IN EDMONTON

My Father's Work

1934 - 1946 - RCNVR

1947 -   BC GOVT PERSONNEL

My Mother's Work

BOOKKEEPER AT DOWELLS CARTAGE

Where Grandmother Was Born

Place Photo Here

I Was Born

When SEPT. 2 1942   Where VICTORIA

I Was Named BERYL LORRAINE

I Weighed

Where Grandfather Was Born

Place Photo Here

I Was Born   IN VIC?

When   JANUARY 28 1941   Where   VICTORIA

I Was Named   RONALD EDWARD

I Weighed

As A Girl

Place Photo Here

My Family Lived _____

I Went to School _____

My Ambition _____

Favourite Things

Song _____

Movie _____ *Actor* _____

Actress _____ *Book* _____

_____

_____

_____

_____

_____

_____

_____

_____

_____

_____

_____

_____

As A Boy

Place Photo Here

My Family Lived

I Went to School

My Ambition

Favourite Things

Song _____

Movie _____ *Actor* _____

Actress _____ *Book* _____

_____

_____

_____

_____

_____

_____

_____

_____

_____

_____

_____

_____

As A Young Woman
FAVOURITE THINGS

Place Photo Here

As A Young Man
FAVOURITE THINGS

Place Photo Here

_____

_____

_____

_____

_____

_____

Our Engagement

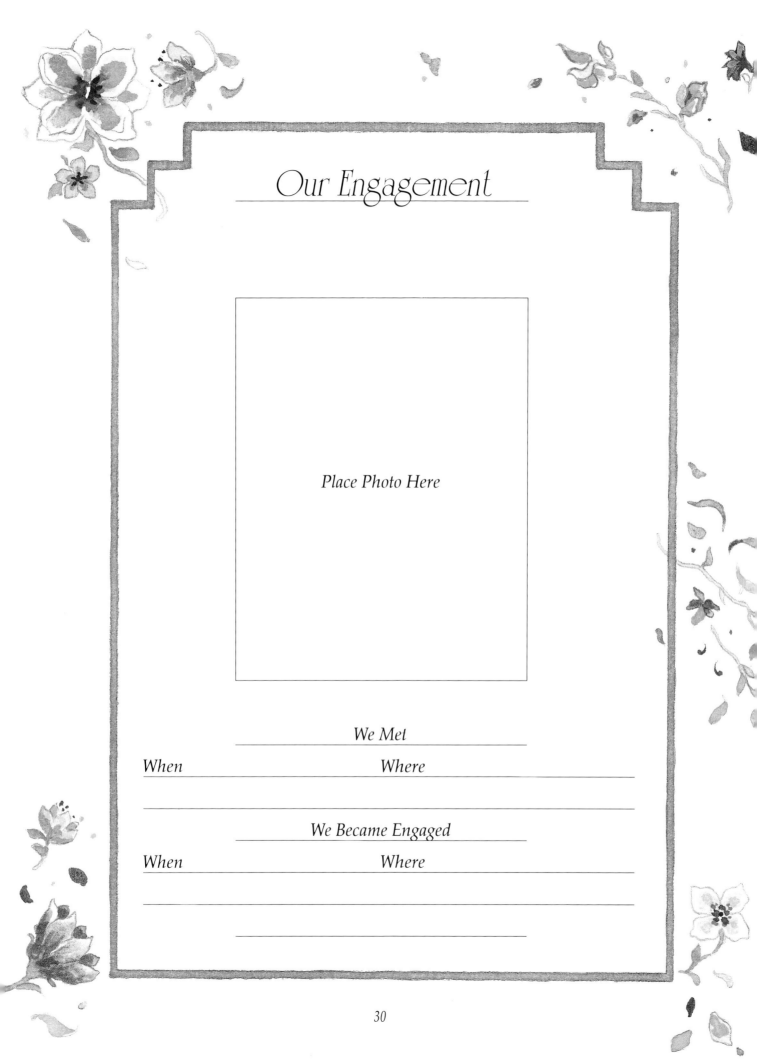

Place Photo Here

We Met

When   *Where*

We Became Engaged

When   *Where*

*Place
Memento
Here*

Our Wedding Day

We Were Married

Date _____ Time _____

Place _____

We Celebrated By

_____

_____

Grandmother Wore

_____

_____

A Memorable Gift

_____

_____

Our Most Vivid Memory

_____

_____

Our Honeymoon

_____

_____

_____

Place Photo Here

Our First Year Of Marriage

We First Lived At

_____

_____

Our Fondest Memory

_____

_____

Grandfather's Job Was

_____

_____

Grandmother's Job Was

_____

_____

We Enjoyed

_____

_____

_____

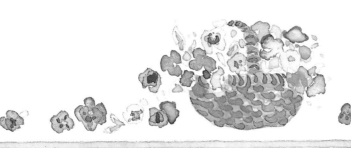

Our First Year Of Marriage

Place Photo Here

Our Child Was Born

Our Child Was Born

When _____ Where _____

We Lived At _____

We Named Our Child

Full Name _____

We Chose That Name Because _____

Colour Of Eyes _____ Colour Of Hair _____

Weight _____ First Word _____

Favourite Toys

_____

_____

Favourite Games

_____

_____

When I Think About The Time

_____

_____

_____

Our Child Was Born

Place Photo Here

Our Child Growing Up

At School

Best Subjects

Showed Talent In

Ambitions

Hobbies

Sports

Our Child Growing Up

Place Photo Here

Place Photo Here

Our Child's Teenage Years

Favourite Music

_____

_____

Favourite Sports

_____

_____

Major Interests

_____

_____

We Were Strict About

_____

_____

We Were Proud That

_____

_____

What We Remember Most

_____

_____

_____

Our Child's Teenage Years

Place Photo Here

Your Parents

They Met

How

When

Where

They Were Married

Date

Place

Your Father Worked As

Your Mother Worked As

Place Photo Here

Your Birth

You Were Born

When   Where

You Weighed

We Thought You Resembled

Your Star Sign

You Were Given The Name

Because

Your Birth

Place Photo Here

Our Earliest Memories Of You

We Remember When You . . .

Place Photo Here

Our Earliest Memories Of You

_____

_____

_____

_____

_____

_____

_____

_____

_____

_____

_____

_____

_____

_____

Our Earliest Memories Of You

Our Earliest Memories Of You

Place Photo Here

Family Reunions

Our Family Gets Together

Place Photo Here

Family Reunions

Our Family

_____ _____

_____ _____

_____ _____

_____ _____

_____ _____

_____ _____

_____ _____

_____ _____

_____ _____

_____ _____

_____ _____

_____ _____

_____ _____

_____ _____

Family Holidays

We Like To Go To

_____

_____

_____

_____

_____

_____

_____

_____

Special Holidays We Shared

_____

_____

_____

Family Heirlooms

_____

_____

_____

_____

_____

_____

_____

_____

_____

_____

_____

_____

Favourite Relatives

Favourite Relatives

Place Photo Here

Place Photo Here

Place Photo Here

Place Photo Here

Place Photo Here

Our Special Memories

We Want You To Know That

_____

_____

_____

_____

_____

_____

_____

_____

_____

_____

_____

_____

Mementoes

Place Favourite Photos
Newspaper Clippings, Mementoes
Here

Mementoes

*Place Favourite Photos
Newspaper Clippings, Mementoes
Here*

Mementoes

Place Favourite Photos
Newspaper Clippings, Mementoes
Here